AF412305

Author:

A simple fellow soul who believes in, completely rational, eternal, and heavenly happiness can be plausible for all. Starting from You!

Irrespective of who we are, it would greatly help us understand the most Reasonable and the most Useful divine concepts like Soul. Importantly, Solutions to Problems based on that profound understanding. Importantly, reap benefits of it, both personally and for all.

We all seek for, more blissful, meaningful, reliable, and sustainable everyday life, starting from our own self. Understanding of the commonly misunderstood, and unclear relationships among all the existences, provide us greatly profound functional wisdom. Logically, it could also be the simplest path for Exponential Pleasure for all.

Reasonable and pure Goodness is Eternal! All the Souls, knowingly and unknowingly, seek for the Eternal Happiness!

Briefly, when we believe in Soul Solutions and act on, it would greatly benefit. In simple, it would be by Respecting and Offering Reasonable Goodness for all, and Rationally Requiring the same from all involved. When it is followed consistently, it would lead to lasting success, peace and pleasure for all.

It is about every single individual's happiness starting from our own self.

We have got All and Beyond to create such blissful state. But the *willingness* of those souls that feasibly can. Also, the contribution of ALL involved, sensibly with No Exceptions. This would accomplish the state of Conclusive Truth - Remarkably Phenomenal and Timeless Happiness.

End of the Soul Solution Search for reasonable common problems and sufferings. The Dawn of the Complete Eternal Bliss for All - Starting from You!

Thank you! Have a Great Day-Every Day!

Sincerely - A Fellow Soul,
Somu Sivaramakrishnan

CONTENTS

Prologue

Welcome and Thank you for joining me in this Conversation. In this short journey with a fellow-soul, let's mutually find out, how a completely reasonable, harmonious, goodness, and happiness filled life can be real and plausible. Not just for Us, but for All Souls, Irrespective of any of our current believes. **Especially, in a profound way, observe, discover, realize, and enjoy that you are the most valuable soul that exists.** Who also deserves the most blissful happiness - in a very profound and positive way.

"Really?!", you may ask.

I think so. Let's very quickly explore.

In brief, profound patterns recommend that all starts from individuals and their own seeking for happiness. Irrespective of the numerous believes that we may have, if we are not here, it would make no sense at all. Assume, if we are not here, we would not even know or realize, the existence of anything here, or anywhere.

Simply, our existence is the most important and our own happiness is the paramount for each of us. How we achieve such, possibly Sustainable Happiness, could differ among us. Still YOU are the most important in this short journey. Right here and right now, you are the one who could deserve the very bests of the eternal bliss - tangibly and profoundly.

Structure of the Book

In this book of, 'Soul Solution Search Series - 101 to 777! Discussion and Solution for common complex questions!', this is Edition 1. This is a **Short Read** Book, that converses on **"Soul"**.

In brief, the Original contents are enriched, appropriately streamlined, and optimized. It is made as mutually beneficial structure of books. You decide what you may prefer for your benefits.

These **Series** of Books are orchestrated and focused for specific reading needs and benefits. **Suite** would include two or more Topics with Questions and Answers (Q&A). Each **Short Book** would discuss about a specific Topic, and would also include Q&A. Where as a **Short Read** is about either a specific Topic or a specific Question, and Serial Numbers will be between 100-999. Further, **Swift Reads** that are Precise contents and Summaries, to the point, with simplified structure and contents. They would have the Serial Numbers between 1000-9999.

Generally, the Contents are in your control, for the pleasure of your reading. **You decide, what is the optimal reading pleasure for you?**

The important point of this framework is, **I Respect Your Time, money and other resources**. I wanted a better Opportunity to serve you, with the Contents that you are interested in and looking for.

Primary Sources of the Contents

Contents of these Series of Books are primarily based on the vast extra ordinary personal experiences and opportunities that I received.

Mostly learned from, wonderful fellow Souls like you. I believe, these books are not completely from me that they are just mine. But these are my Interpretations of that I learned in my This Life. Further, throughout **Life of my Soul's** humbly well-read, for lack of terms, in **The Curriculum of my Soul**. The true education, I received from the truly-countless, all the souls that I encountered. Like You, and like this book. Now, in a way, in the **Calling of my Soul**, I am seeking to learn from wonderful Souls like You. Also, share some of my Unique and Useful ideas that can enrich mutual Happiness for all.

Learning from Experiences that are both terribly also awfully bad, and wonderfully also blissfully great. I am very Thankful for all the wealth of experiences. Though, I greatly prefer those that make the situation better for all involved. More importantly, Self motivated Soul Solution Search for specific problems, and self-interpretations of everyday wisdom from all fellow-souls like you. My heartily honor, appreciation, and Thank you.

Further, if anyone finds any of the content as inappropriate in anyways, please forgive me. Please note that the intent of the content is to promote Reasonable, Sustainable, Completely Inclusive - Goodness based Happiness for All.

Acknowledgements

*Thanks for my **Parents** for bringing me to this Great World,*

*Thanks for my Great **Friends** for teaching me to Think Good,*

*Thanks for my **Family** for their extended support during Toughest Times,*

*and **Special Thanks for You** for accompanying me in this Brief Journey!*

*Also, my Thanks for Everyone, Everything & Nothing - **All the Souls!***

Soul

Dear Good Soul. Foremost, Thank you for accompanying me in this brief journey.

"Really?! How do you even know that I am a Good Soul?", you may ask.

Well, as we start this brief journey, where I know nothing about you. I wanted to positively assume something Good about you. So, I assumed and addressed you as Good Soul. I call this Positive-Prejudge-Enabling for the ease and please of the conversations.

Life that is made up of such pleasant simple things as, Thinking someone Good and Thanking someone for even small things. It makes the journey more beautiful and delightful. Feeling Thankful, sharing and expressing make it greatly pleasing for everyone involved. For the most, it ensures, enables and empowers to be happier, than if just be based on the materialistic circumstances.

Soul! Assume that your body is sitting comfortably and reading this book. If not, please make yourself comfortable. The environment is safe, at least some peace in mind, and reasonable for you. Thank you.

Now, when you comfortably read, your body is apparent and tangible. But someone is reading along with you that only you can realize. May be you call your consciousness or your self or any other names you may want to call. The part of you that is not physical, but had been, and will be with you FOREVER! For simplicity, let us call him / her / other as Soul - for now.

If you are an enquiring, empathetic, and compassionate soul, you can understand it better. If you cannot for now, do not worry. You will ultimately. Mostly, it cannot be expressed through articulation, but can only be understood through profound inner realizations.

It is too insightful that it cannot easily to be explained to one another. More importantly, it is hard for anyone to ever make you Feel and Realize, it for yourselves in its Entirety. Gradually, you will know it for yourself.

Irrespective of who we are, it would be greatly fruitful to know about Souls. It would need open minded willingness, efforts, practices, and karma, to know it at reasonable level in this lifetime. It would be hard to make someone really teach, enable to realize, evaluate and understand it without one's own longing for it. If some one could, it would be very rare, through one of Truly Enlightened or trending to Great Souls.

It would be based on such Great Souls who display True and Explicit Values, and Practices - Not just through read knowledge. It is not just about knowledge, but primarily about Reasonable Practice. We need to be aware though, in recognizing a Good or a Great or an Enlightened Soul, from a less-than-standard soul.

No need for any compelling complex-sacrilege tests. But some basic levels of willingness and openness in the Good Soul conversation. It would be without need for, any negatively - comparing, conflicting, or concluding on one's views are better than the other's. Rather, through complacent mutual complements. Just pure seeking, asking, listening, possible mutual learning, consuming, benefiting, enjoying, and finally Thanking for each other.

Good Souls like us, start with believing in the other souls as Genuinely Good Souls. This positive-prejudge or assumptions greatly help us toward positively motivated results. At the same time, our Goodness and positive expectations could place us in some trouble. As it sometimes also give a few overly materialistic souls to take advantage of, in wrongful ways.

We must not think too much about the negativity irrationally. At the same time, we just need to be little more aware of such souls and scenarios. Further, quickly navigate to our Reasonable, Positive and Beneficial ways of living for all. It would be including those with negativities.

Understanding of souls could be the easiest when like minded souls interact. Otherwise, it could be extremely hard, strive to understand - even with complete determination, openness, and freewill. As it is not just about reading and understanding. But more importantly, requiring feeling beyond normal perceptions, presumptions, and practices.

Basic levels of fairness and empathy towards other souls, without constraints, felt and understood would greatly help. Understanding of such souls could be easier, otherwise could be extremely complex. For now, let us believe that your beliefs on the souls are the best - at least for yourself, and so their own for everyone. Let us be Content and Happy with it for now - peace for all in mind.

In certain, heavenly presence you could naturally be enabled to Feel and Understand the Soul for yourselves. Also some heavily pressured circumstances may also permit us tap into. In this case, we could understand the soul to some level. Apparently, one way is always preferred than the other.

Numerous diversified teachings and perceptions make understanding of the Souls more complicated. For example, some believe that the sinful Souls will vanish after life. Some others believe that the Blissful Souls will become one into peace.

Indeed, very complicated to comprehend. Especially because of the preconceptions, understanding, and complexities involved.

Common beliefs and assumptions that involve are vast. Further, unprecedented levels of diverse, and unclear premises to be navigated. As example,

* Souls are progressed after life by means of credentials, that lead to Heaven or

* The value of cumulative learning and accomplishments through unknown and uncountable lives. It is the profound Tests and Travel. That believed to end based on, the at most state of value that can be attained. Then it would eternally end, by becoming as part of the God Himself or Herself or Itself.

* Also sometimes conceived to become one with Nature, Everything and Nothing.

Complex for sure, if without some levels of, related knowledge and understanding.

* Just collective values of deeds, for known and unknown reasons. They are spent in this life that we live in. As we feel and know - right here and right now, or more deeply

* An Atom to the Universe and everything in between as we know in this life and beyond, known and unknown. They all have individual and collective Souls that Ever Exists. Every Soul has its Profound and Inconceivable Value. Cumulative Experience and Knowledge from an Ever Living Soul is Permanently Obscure during this life. A Soul's Value can only be, retrieved limited and understood hazily, for purposefully unknown reasons.

Relevant and fractional Soul's values are repossessed and forgotten during related triggers during this life. Even for non-beings. At freewill and importantly accidentally, a Soul's value can be enriched through a life time of Goodness produced. It is especially kept unknown for Good reasons.

A Soul's value could change based on ever single even inconceivable little deeds and things that occur. As result, subatomic level consequences and domino effects are evaluated and calculated that are Complete. The Completeness of the calculations and protecting them are beyond life as we know it. The methods of calculations used are unimaginable and haze at best.

There is simplicity in this complex context of understanding of the Souls. It is that, just by being **Reasonably and Consistently Good could fetch all the bliss.** It could reward with unthinkably greater eternal happiness. In this conception, all is very well captured and recorded. In its entirety utilized for more Good to be produced for now and beyond this life. In brief, **What goes around Exponentially comes around with complete reasoning!** Or Simply

* Rejected as, "There is nothing as Soul exists at all", or many more such - BELIEFs!

They are just BELIEFs that could be diversified and difficult to realize. Especially, it is hard to understand, from the perspectives of the others. In extreme circumstances, for some closed individuals and groups, understanding could further be exceedingly hard. It is because they are not simplified for them.

Also, sometimes they do not allow, entertain or believe in such opportunities. Because for simple self satisfaction, worry of punishment for considered sacrilege, or the benefit of very small groups who seldom even benefit from it. So, it is still hard and unnecessarily-complex for the unfortunate-innocents. When referred with respect, empathy and Goodness.

Ultimately, it supposed to be meaningful-differences of various kinds. Instead of supporting and benefiting towards broadened-blessed-blissfulness, as misunderstood, it unfortunately hurts the mutual-harmony.

For some, it may seem like the discussion on the Soul somehow tending to discuss on religion. It is common perception. They both are in general discussed mostly related and have similar kinds of scenarios applicable. So it could be perceived in such way.

When it gets to religion, in general, it gets more intensive. It is a common and reasonable understanding that Good Souls believe and support mutual respect and acceptance. Especially, keeping precious personal beliefs respectfully with in. At the same time, respecting others ideas, either understood, misunderstood or amalgamated.

Beliefs are reasonably, respected, and accepted by Good Souls. Provided it can reasonably produce goodness without creating conflicts. Also, make someone feel hurt as sacrilege to their reasonable beliefs, intention to deceive, or such below standard acts.

Good human souls also believe in Soul, God, Religion, and such divineness. They also believe that their beliefs offer great common values and goodness. It is not considered a big barrier for them to comfort, love and help those with other beliefs.

For such Good Souls, it is respectful and acceptable, when an idea can deliver Goodness and Happiness for all. Though they may heartily praise and love, their own beloved God and Religion that bring eventual pleasant structure in to their lives.

Different believes preach different ideas, based on its own evolution, and countless historic circumstances. Good souls take the reasonable goodness from it. A simple starting solution towards mutual understanding, harmony and happiness could be, to simply respect each others beliefs.

Initially some might be worried to respect others beliefs as they praise and protect their own beliefs. This is completely reasonable and understandable. If we truly wish that our own beliefs to be understood, respected and praised by others then at least understandably we need to be assistive.

For mutual harmony and fruitfulness, it would be reasonable that we may also be willing to be flexible in a supportive way. It is not that one to follow the other. But for eventual and considerable mutual benefits, both to just respect each others views harmoniously.

Ultimately, the informed souls would recognize that all different beliefs are tending to, in the end towards, ideas for happier life experience. If you will such happiness even beyond life as we could feel and know it.

When discussed, it is believed by the Good Souls that some of simple, good, and diversified knowledge profoundly helps. Understanding and using them in every day life, contributes, comforts, and evolves their own good beliefs, at various levels. It enriches towards more profound and eternally genuine Goodness, and Happiness.

Eventually, for different individuals, the level at which it could be understood, and felt might vary. It would be based on the circumstances and the understanding of the individual that seeks, or the group that discusses.

Especially, the understanding and benefit would be higher, when such discussion can be genuinely open and sensible. Ultimately, it would more beneficially progress them, in their own beliefs with more reasoning and respect.

Progressing to Profound Happiness!

Thank you!

Have a Great Day - Every Day!